POTUS 2024

The road to the white house

Celine Morgan

Table of content

Introduction

The 2024 American Presidential Election carries unprecedented weight, embodying a critical juncture in the nation's history. Against a backdrop of global challenges, economic shifts, and societal transformations, the electorate faces decisions that transcend mere political transitions. As the nation grapples with the consequences of a pandemic, climate concerns, and evolving cultural dynamics, the outcome of this election will determine not only the occupant of the highest office but also the trajectory of policies that resonate domestically and internationally.

It stands as a pivotal moment where citizens shape the course of their country, influencing its stance on crucial issues from healthcare to foreign relations. In 2024, voters bear the responsibility of steering America's path amid complexities, making this election a defining chapter in the ongoing narrative of the nation.

Chapter 1

Historical Context and Previous Elections

America's democratic ideals and changing political climate have molded the country's rich and varied electoral history. Since George Washington became the nation's first president in 1788, when he was unanimously chosen, the United States has conducted regular presidential elections. Over time, the election process has undergone substantial modifications that are indicative of both societal changes and constitutional reforms.

The passage of the 15th Amendment in 1870, which guaranteed the right to vote to all people regardless of race, was a significant turning point in electoral history. Due to discriminatory measures like poll fees and literacy exams, African Americans were not fully enfranchised for several decades.

Reforms including secret ballots and direct primary elections were introduced in the late 19th and early 20th centuries. The goal of these modifications was to increase the voting process's inclusivity and transparency.

The 19th Amendment, which gave women the right to vote, was ratified in the 1920s. The Civil Rights Movement in later decades resulted in the Voting Rights Act of 1965, which outlawed discriminatory voting practices directed towards minority groups.

Election campaigns were changed by television's introduction in the middle of the 20th century, which made it possible for candidates to connect with more people. The presidential candidates' televised debates turned into important landmarks that shaped voters' opinions.

Concerns over the influence of technology on elections and the reform of campaign funding have gained importance in the last few decades. For example, the impact of social media has altered the nature of political campaigning and communication.

Among the notable elections are the highly contested 2000 race between George W. Bush and Al Gore, which the Supreme Court ultimately decided. As the first African American president, Barack Obama's victory in 2008 was a historic occasion that represented advancements in racial relations.

Unconventional campaigning was used in the 2016 election, when Donald Trump defeated Hillary Clinton in the electoral college. Amid the problems provided by the COVID-19 outbreak, Joe Biden defeated Trump in the next 2020 election.

Elections have always been a vital means of expressing popular opinion, creating public policy, and tracking the development of the country. Elections continue to be a mainstay of the American political system because of the continuous dedication to democratic values.

Electoral College

The Electoral College was created as a compromise between the framers of the Constitution who wanted the president to be chosen by Congress and those who preferred a national popular vote. Article Two of the Constitution originally established the system of presidential elections.

According to Article Two, every state is given the same number of electors as its total number of delegates in both chambers of Congress. Following the Twenty-Third Amendment's passage in 1961, the District of Columbia was awarded electors equivalent to those allotted to the state with the fewest citizens. Nevertheless, U.S. territories are not represented in the Electoral College since they are not given electors.

State Legislatures

According to Article II, Section 1, Clause 2 of the state constitution, electors are chosen "in such Manner as the Legislature Thereof May Direct" by the legislature of each state. Just six of the eleven states that were eligible to vote in the first presidential election (1789) selected electors through popular vote.

The states gradually started holding popular elections to select their slate of electors throughout time. Just five of the sixteen states selected their electors through popular vote in 1800; this number rose dramatically to eighteen out of twenty-four states by 1824, with the emergence of Jacksonian democracy.The number of states that choose electors through popular vote increased dramatically to 18 out of 24. The franchise's property limits gradually decreased in tandem with this gradual shift towards more democratisation. Only South Carolina, out of the 26 states, continued to have its state legislature choose electors by 1840.

Vice presidents

Eligible voters selected one of two presidential candidates under the original Article Two system. The winner of the most votes (assuming that they accounted for a majority of the electoral votes) was declared the president, and the runner-up was declared the vice president. This caused an issue in the 1800 presidential contest when Aaron Burr, who had the same amount of electoral votes as Thomas Jefferson, ran against Jefferson for the presidency. Alexander Hamilton's clout in the House ultimately led to the selection of Jefferson as president.

The Twelfth Amendment was enacted in reaction to the 1800 election, forcing electors to cast separate ballots for the president and vice president. Although this resolved the immediate issue, it diminished the standing of the vice presidency as the front-runner for the presidency was no longer in that position. When popular elections began to determine a state's Electoral College delegation later in the 19th century, the separate ballots for president and vice president were rendered mostly moot. Pledged to vote for a specific presidential and vice presidential candidate (provided by the same political party) are electors selected in this manner. Despite being technically elected separately,in practice they are chosen together.

Tie vote

Rules for the case that no candidate receives a majority of the Electoral College votes are likewise set by the Twelfth Amendment. Andrew Jackson won a plurality of the electoral votes voted in the 1824 presidential election, but not a majority of them. John Quincy Adams was victorious as the winner of the House-conducted election. Andrew Jackson and House Speaker Henry Clay, who had also run for office, developed a strong rivalry.

There was no need for the Senate to vote on a vice presidential nominee because John Calhoun, the nominee for vice president, earned the majority of votes after running on both the Jackson and Adams tickets.

Popular vote

With the exception of the sporadic "faithless elector," the popular vote has been used since 1824 to determine the electoral vote, which in turn decides the electoral college vote for each state or district and, ultimately, the outcome of a presidential election. While there is no direct correlation between the national popular vote and the outcome of a presidential election, it does have a substantial influence.

The victor of the national popular vote has also won the Electoral College vote in 54 of the 59 elections that have been held so far, or almost 91% of the total. Only in close elections have the Electoral College and national popular vote winners diverged.In very competitive elections, politicians do not attempt to maximize their popular vote by means of actual or fraudulent vote gains in one-party areas; instead, they concentrate on garnering support in the contested swing states that are essential to securing an electoral college majority. Nonetheless, there have been presidential candidates who have won despite not receiving the most votes in the countrywide popular vote. Jackson prevailed in the popular vote in the 1824 election, although no candidate secured a majority of electoral votes.The Twelfth Amendment mandates that the House select the winner of the presidential election from among the top three candidates. After finishing in fourth place, Clay threw his support behind Adams, who went on to win. Jackson's supporters said that Adams won the presidency by working with Clay since Adams then made Clay his secretary of state. Allegations of a "corrupt bargain" persisted during Adams' presidency.

Chapter 2

A comparison of the totals of the popular vote since 1900.

Democrat and Republican

Together, all other contenders
The electoral vote winner in five presidential elections
(1824, 1876, 1888, 2000, and 2016) was an outright
loser in the popular vote.Though many constitutional
amendments have been proposed, none of them have
ever been able to pass both Houses of Congress in
order to replace the Electoral College with a direct
popular vote. The National Popular Vote Interstate
Compact is a further alternative plan that would require
participating states to agree to distribute electors based
on the outcome of the national popular vote rather than
only their particular statewide outcomes.

Election date

The variables (weather, harvests, and worship) led to
the establishment of Tuesday as the presidential
election day in November. Tuesday was a great day to
vote when voters still went to the polls on horseback
since it allowed them to vote on Tuesday, before market
day on Wednesday, and pray on Sunday, then ride to
their county seat on Monday. November also falls
comfortably between the harvest season and the hard

winter cold, which could be particularly detrimental for horse-and-buggy travelers.

Electoral Count Act of 1887

Main Article : Election Count Act

In reaction to the contentious 1876 election, in which many states submitted opposing slates of electors, Congress created the Electoral Count Act in 1887. Procedures for the electoral vote count were set by legislation. Title 3 of the United States Code now has a codification of it. It also contains a "safe harbour" deadline by which states are required to settle any disputes regarding the electorate selection in the end.

Inauguration day

Because it took so long to count and report the votes and because it was logistically difficult for the victor to get to the capital, presidents were not sworn in until March 4 until 1937. Presidential inaugurations were shifted to 20 January at noon, allowing presidents to begin office earlier, thanks to advancements in transportation and the ratification of the Twentieth Amendment.

Campaign spending

The purpose of the Federal Election Campaign Act of 1971 was to improve donation disclosure for federal campaigns. Following legal modifications, candidates for federal offices are now required to file a Statement of Candidature with the Federal Election Commission prior to accepting contributions totaling more than $5,000 or incurring expenses totaling more than $5,000. As a result, it became common for presidential candidates to announce their plans to run as early as the spring of the year before in order to begin raising and allocating the funds required for their national campaigns.

Political parties

George Washington, the first president, won the election as an independent. Every American president since John Adams was elected in 1796 has come from one of the country's two major parties. Only twice have third parties finished second—in 1860 and 1912. The last time a third-party candidate gained any electoral votes from voters who weren't disloyal was George Wallace Figures. The last time a third-party candidate saw considerable success (even though they still came in third place) was Ross Perot in 1992.

Overview of major political parties

Democratic Party

American Democratic Party and its History
One of the two main political parties in the United States
is the Democratic Party. It is the world's oldest remaining
voter-based political party, having been established as
the Democratic Party in 1828 by Andrew Jackson and
Martin Van Buren.

Regarding domestic matters, the Democratic Party has
positioned itself as the liberal party since 1912. Since
1932, the party's programme has been heavily affected
by Franklin D. Roosevelt's economic ideology, which
has had a significant impact on contemporary American
liberalism.
Except for President Eisenhower's two terms from 1953
to 1961, Roosevelt's New Deal alliance ruled the White
House until 1968. The Democratic Party was the most
popular party among white southerners up until the
middle of the 20th century, and it was also the one most
closely linked to the upholding of slavery.
 The Democratic Party became the more progressive
party on civil rights issues with Lyndon B. Johnson's
Great Society, and they would gradually lose power in
the southern states until 1996. Democrats have
generally supported social justice, social liberalism, a

mixed economy, and the welfare state since the middle of the 20th century; however, Bill Clinton and other New Democrats have advocated for free trade and neoliberalism, which is thought to have influenced public opinion.

Democrats are most prevalent in the Northeast, West Coast, and large American cities in the twenty-first century. Trade unions and Latinos and African-Americans are disproportionately Democratic. With 72 million registered voters (42.6% of 169 million registered voters) declaring affiliation in 2004, it was the largest political party. Barack Obama became president in 2009 and remained in office until January 2017, despite his party's 2004 loss in the presidential election. Obama was the fifteenth Democrat to occupy the position. The Democratic Party also had the majority in the US Senate from the 2006 midterm elections to the 2014 midterm elections.

According to a 2011 USA Today analysis of state voter rolls, there has been a decrease in the number of Democrats registered in 25 out of 28 states (other jurisdictions do not register voters based on party). Republican registrants fell over this period, coinciding with an increase in independent or no preference votes. The number of Democrats fell by 800,000 in 2011 and by 1.7 million, or 3.9%, from 2008.[65] The Democratic Party had almost 60 million registered members in 2018, making it the largest in the US.

Republican Party

The United States Republican Party and its historical background
One of the two main modern political parties in the US is the Republican Party. Though it is younger than the Democratic Party, it has been dubbed the "Grand Old Party" (GOP) by the media since the 1880s. Founded in 1854 by modernizers and anti-slavery militants in the North, the Republican Party gained notoriety in 1860 after Abraham Lincoln was elected and utilized the party apparatus to help win the American Civil War.

During the Third Party System (1854–1896) and the Fourth Party System (1896–1932), the Republican Party controlled American politics. The Republican Party has been the more market-oriented of the two American political parties since the early 20th century, frequently supporting measures that support the interests of American corporations. This party has a history of supporting stronger national defense policies and bettering veteran's benefits because it was formerly founded on the votes of Union Army veterans.

The Republican Party currently espouses an American conservative agenda that is further grounded in social conservatism, fiscal conservatism, and economic liberalism.

In the United States, the Republican Party is more prevalent in the South and in less centralized, lower-density portions of large urban centers [68].[69] The Republican Party had controlled the United States House of Representatives since the 2010 midterm elections; however, they were defeated by the Democratic Party in the 2018 midterm elections. In addition, the Republican Party dominated the Senate from the elections of 2014 until the 2020 elections. With almost 55 million registered members in 2018, the Republican Party was the second-largest in the US. Following the 2020 US elections, the Republican Party lost its senate majority, and Chuck Schumer was named Senate Majority Leader as part of a power-sharing arrangement with the GOP.

Existential concerns are expected to gain prominence in discussions on everything from the future of reproductive rights to the likelihood of taking significant action on climate change, the extent of US support for Ukraine in its conflict with Russia, and the future of democracy in America.

Economy

Stupidly, it's the economy. In 1992, James Carville, a Democratic strategist and Bill Clinton advisor, made this statement. The majority of Americans believed that the economy's stewardship should change: Clinton defeated George H.W. Bush, the incumbent president.

Under Joe Biden, the post-Covid recovery appears to be proceeding as planned, nearly thirty years later. While the Dow is at an all-time high, unemployment is low. That should be encouraging for Biden, but the real question is whether enough people in the United States believe that the economy is robust or that it is specifically benefiting them. Many, it appears, do not. Public surveys are dominated by questions on cost of living, and inflation is still high. Republican threats to Medicare and social security might counteract such concerns, which is why Biden and Donald Trump have seized upon any indication that a Republican candidate (Nicki Haley, for example) might be a threat to these programmes.

Republican threats to Medicare and social security might counteract such concerns, which is why Biden and Donald Trump have seized upon any indication that a Republican candidate (Nicki Haley, for example) might be a threat to these programmes.

Equality

Attacks on LGBTQ+ rights have been a defining feature of Ron DeSantis's campaign to "Make America Florida." The conservative governor's disastrous campaign indicates how effectively that has failed, but it is important to acknowledge Republican attempts to demonize all manifestations of so-called "woke" philosophy. There have been observable outcomes, such as anti-trans laws, restrictions on LGBTQ+ issues in schools and book bans, and the elimination of racial affirmative action in university admissions because of the conservative majority on the Supreme Court.

Traditional racialized issues will continue to play a customary role on the campaign trail, especially as Trump deploys extreme "blood and soil" rhetoric in front of eager crowds. This is demonstrated by the ongoing struggles over immigration on Capitol Hill and Republicans' usual focus on crime in large cities. Meanwhile, a very concerning indication for the

Democrats is that Black and Hispanic support for Biden is no longer a given.

Abortion

Leading Democrats have made it plain that their party will target Republican assaults on abortion rights, including the extreme restrictions in Republican-held states and the candidates who support them, as well as the Dobbs v. Jackson Supreme Court decision that overturned Roe v. Wade last year and the impending Mifepristone case.
For Democrats, it makes tactical sense because, since Dobbs was handed down, the party has obviously gained a number of electoral victories, even in conservative states, and the danger to women's reproductive rights is a rare subject on which the party polls quite high.

But even as he attempts to absolve himself of responsibility for nominating three judges who voted to overturn Roe, Trump is obviously aware of how powerful the topic is. Inquiries concerning their medical histories and abortion intentions have been avoided by Haley and DeSantis. They can anticipate constant attacks from the Republican candidate, whoever they may be.

Foreign policy

The Israel-Gaza conflict poses a formidable challenge for Biden: how to appease or at the very least appease the Israel lobby as well as sizable segments of his own party, especially the left and the younger members who are more pro-Palestinian.

Growing demonstrations against Israel's bombardment of Gaza and the West Bank highlight the risk of a breakdown at the base. Republicans celebrated a political win during a recent Capitol Hill hearing when the University of Pennsylvania's president resigned due to accusations of antisemitism during student demonstrations for Palestinian rights.

In other news, Biden is still in charge of an international alliance that backs Ukraine in its conflict with Russia, but Republicans who want harsh immigration reform are preventing further US funding, and some of them are eager to give up on Kyiv completely. During the election year, there will undoubtedly be a lot of discussion about foreign policy due to the lingering effects of the chaotic withdrawal from Afghanistan (which Trump engineered but Biden botched), uncertainties about what the US should do in the event that China attacks Taiwan, and the threat that Trump poses to US membership in NATO.

Democracy

If Biden is content to be viewed as a champion of democracy overseas, he is becoming more and more eager to draw attention to the dangers facing democracy at home. After all, his most likely rival has stated he wants to be a "dictator" from day one, has refused to recognise the outcome of the 2020 election, encouraged the deadly attack on Congress on January 6, 2021, and has been connected to plans to reduce the federal government in a second term

Trump will undoubtedly continue to assert the falsehood that electoral fraud caused his defeat in 2020 even as 17 of the 91 state and federal cases pertaining to election subversion are headed for trial. In the polls, Biden has found the topic to be profitable. However, DeSantis and Haley have to skirt the issue in order to appease Trump fans. The New York Times provides a depressing summary of their answers as follows: DeSantis has put limits on voting rights in Florida and has refrained from discussing 2020 issues for a while, while Haley has acknowledged that Biden's win was valid but has elevated the possibility of widespread voter fraud.

Climate

The US itself is at risk from the climate problem, if Trump continues to attack US democracy. Climate change is undeniably real, as evidenced by events like devastating floods, hurricanes, and forest fires. Public surveys confirm this: Remarkably, half of Republicans, or 70% of Americans, desire significant action. However, this isn't evident in Republican campaign messaging. Trump claims he opposes initiatives to increase the use of clean energy and doesn't think human activity causes climate change or that it exacerbates extreme weather.

CHAPTER 3

Explanation of Primary Elections and Caucus System

What are caucuses and primaries?

First things first:

Primaries are not caucuses. State political party members congregate in a presidential caucus to choose delegates to represent them at a state convention for presidential nominations. These face-to-face meetings can go on for hours, during which time participants engage in heated debates to persuade one another of the virtues of their chosen candidate.

States, not political parties, are in charge of hosting primaries. A primary is an election; it does not necessitate that participants congregate in one location at one time. In an indirect primary, voters choose delegates to represent their favourite candidate in a statewide party convention, or they can choose candidates directly, depending on the state.

The history of caucuses

Although they didn't look exactly like they do now, caucuses were common in the early history of the United States. Both parties started using a covert caucus of US congressmen to nominate presidential candidates in 1796; this arrangement is known as the "King Caucus." However, in 1824, a number of presidential contenders declined to ask King Caucus for his approval on the grounds of principle, and municipal caucuses quickly took its place. These state caucuses, which began in the 1840s, were the norm for selecting presidential candidates before a national party convention.

However, there was a drawback to these caucuses as well: a select few party insiders typically held most of the power. Local caucuses were dominated by party bosses, therefore in order to get the nomination, national contenders had to assemble alliances with state and local bosses.

Reformers of the Progressive era promoted primary elections in the 1890s as a means of democratising the presidential nomination process by giving regular people a direct platform to express their political opinions. Twenty-five states had moved to primaries by 1916. However, party executives continued to control national conventions in spite of reform, frequently ignoring primary results and selecting candidates on their own.

Subsequently, the Democratic Party established the McGovern-Fraser Commission to recommend new guidelines for the party's upcoming convention following the turbulent 1968 Democratic National Convention, which produced Hubert Humphrey's nomination despite his lack of participation in any primary elections. Reform was sparked by the commission's recommendations in both parties: The primary system was implemented by the majority of state parties starting with the 1972 election.
But not in Iowa, where supporters of the state's long-standing caucus system contend that the process is intrinsically more democratic than primaries.

Modern caucuses

In contrast to the past, when party executives held secret meetings, caucuses today unite regular people to choose their favourite candidates. In order to demonstrate their viability on the national stage, prospective presidents need to win these people in Iowa, which is the first state on the calendar for candidate nominations, along with the New Hampshire primary. According to Tara Golshan and Ella Nilsen for Vox, a candidate can win in Iowa with very little votes since there are so many contenders running early in the nomination process that the vote is automatically split. Candidates frequently withdraw from the race after receiving a trouncing in the state.

The group of presidential electors that the US Constitution mandates meet every four years to elect the country's president and vice president is known as the Electoral College. In accordance with the procedures outlined by its law, each state selects electors, which are equal in number to their congressional delegation (senators and representatives).As per a 1961 amendment, the federal District of Columbia is likewise endowed with three electors. Senators and congressmen, among others, who hold federal offices, are not eligible to vote. To elect the president and vice president, a simple majority of 270 electoral votes or more are needed out of the 538 electors currently in office. The House of Representatives holds a contingent election to choose the president, and the Senate holds a contingency election to choose the vice president, in the event that no candidate wins a majority there.

On Election Day in November, the states and the District of Columbia hold a statewide or district-wide popular vote to select electors based on their pledges to vote for the president and vice president; certain state laws forbid electors from being disloyal.every state but Maine and Nebraska selects two electors for the ticket with the largest statewide vote in addition to one elector for each congressional district. The president and vice president are sworn in in January after the electors convene and cast their votes in December.

The United States, which came closest to moving to direct presidential elections in 1969–70, continues to dispute the benefits of the electoral college system. While detractors contend that it is not indicative of the country's public will, supporters contend that winning needs presidential candidates to have widespread appeal across the nation.
The idea of "one person, one vote" is not in line with winner-take-all systems, particularly when representation is not proportionate to population.Opponents point out the unfairness that gives individual residents in smaller states more voting power than residents in larger states because of the distribution of electors.This is due to the fact that each state appoints as many electors as the size of its congressional delegation, all states, regardless of population, are entitled to a minimum of three electors, and the distribution of the remaining, statutorily determined number is only loosely proportionate. This distribution helped the national popular vote runners-up to win the presidency in 1824, 1876, 1888, 2000, and 2016. Furthermore, voters who lack faith may not cast their ballots according to their promises.

Candidates

Democrats

Bidin

Following the turmoil of the Trump administration, President Biden has positioned himself as a defender of democracy and a unifying force.

He is anticipated to run on a platform of bipartisan achievements, such as a significant infrastructure plan, and Democratic ideals, such as abortion rights, which Republicans vehemently oppose. Many Democrats are concerned about him because he is the oldest president to compete for reelection, but the party has publicly put those concerns aside and unified behind him.

Marianne Williamson

A self-help writer and former Oprah Winfrey spiritual advisor is a candidate seeking reelection a second term.

She advocated for a federal Department of Peace, backed racial reparations, and described Trumpism as a sign of a psychological disorder in Americans that could not be treated by political measures during her failed 2020 campaign. She has also supported questionable or

refuted medical hypotheses, especially those related to
mental illness.

Dean Phillips

Despite not having many significant ideological
differences with President Biden and having backed his
legislative agenda, a moderate Democrat who was
elected to the House in 2018 feels that the party need to
select someone else due to Mr. Biden's advanced age
and poor popularity.

A former chairman of Talenti Gelato and the heir to a
Minnesota spirits company, Mr Phillips resigned from a
leadership role in the Democratic House to pursue his
dream of running for president, defying the desires of
the majority of the party's elected representatives.

Republicans

Donald J.Trump

In an attempt to regain the presidency that he lost in
2020, former President Donald J. Trump has gone so far
as to incite a crowd of his fans to storm the US Capitol.

He still has a sizable and devoted fan base, and even though his influence within the Republican Party has somewhat decreased (and he is being investigated by both the Justice Department and state authorities), he may benefit in the 2024 primary from a number of opponents who will divide the small anti-Trump vote.

Nikki Haley

A former South Carolina governor and Mr. Trump's UN ambassador, she has highlighted her life experience as the daughter of Indian immigrants and positioned herself as part of "a new generation of leadership."

Although she called for the removal of the Confederate battle flag from the grounds of the South Carolina Capitol in 2015, she was long regarded as a rising Republican star who could avoid extremes and still win over core supporters. However, her popularity within the party has decreased as a result of her intermittent support for Mr. Trump.

Ryan Binkley

is a pastor in a Texas church as well as the president of a mergers and acquisitions company. He has never previously held or campaigned for public office.

On his website, Mr. Binkley asserts that "the problems we face, and the blame we lay, can all be rectified if we look to God, find the good in our fellow Americans, and resolve to trust each other one more time." Binkley positions himself as a "unifying" candidate who can transcend political divisions. Two of his main policy recommendations are to balance the federal budget in seven years and to reform immigration.

Ron De Santis

Ron De Santis has established a reputation around the country as a fierce conservative who is not afraid to take on liberals.

In his capacity as governor of Florida, he oversaw a lax response to the coronavirus outbreak and, with the support of a supportive state legislature, he restricted the teaching of racial history in schools and implemented significant laws that impacted LGBT+ Floridians. In addition, he has frequently used the executive branch to subdue political opponents, ranging from Disney to a local Democratic prosecutor.

Robert F. Kennedy Jr.

Robert F. Kennedy Jr. is a well-known opponent of vaccinations and the nephew of former President John F. Kennedy. Before declaring in October that he would run as an independent, he first sought the Democratic nomination.

He has championed refuted allegations that vaccines given to children cause autism and blasted mandatory coronavirus vaccination programmes and other efforts to prevent pandemics; he even likened them to Nazi Germany, a move for which he later issued an apology. Having previously worked as an environmental lawyer to help clean up the Hudson River, his anti-vaccine campaign has caused pain to his close-knit political family.

Cornel West

Cornel West is a philosophy professor at Union Theological Seminary. He has taught at Yale, Princeton, and Harvard. His leftist activity is well-known, and he has been known to criticise former President Barack Obama harshly.
At first, Dr. West declared he would compete for the People's Party, a third party headed by a former Senator Bernie Sanders campaign staffer. He later declared that he would run as an independent but later changed his mind and declared that he would instead seek the Green Party's candidature.

Physician Jill Stein

Physician Jill Stein is vying for the party's candidature for a third time. She campaigned for president on the Green Party platform in both 2012 and 2016.
She advocated for a "economic bill of rights" in a video launching her campaign, which would guarantee everyone the right to work, health care, housing, food, and education. She also emphasised her support for halting climate change, defending the rights of transgender people, and abortion.

Swing States

Swing states are ones where either contender has a chance to win in the US presidential election. These states, sometimes referred to as "battleground states," are where presidential contenders concentrate their efforts and financial resources during the campaign.

Their opposites are referred to be "safe states," wherein pre-election opinion polls predict that a given party's nominee will almost certainly win. Therefore, during the election campaign, safe states are not given priority when it comes to time and money allocation.

Debate

Presidential Debate, Texas State University, San Marcos, September 16.
At Lafayette College in Easton, Pennsylvania, on September 25. (discussion on the vice president).
The presidential debate is scheduled for October 1 at Virginia State University in Petersburg, Virginia.
October 9 at the presidential debate at the University of Utah in Salt Lake City, Utah.
Candidates must be eligible under the constitution, appear on enough ballots to gain a majority of electoral votes, and receive an average of at least 15% in nationwide surveys conducted by groups the commission has chosen in order to be considered for the debates.[255] Kennedy now has the polling percentages necessary to appear on stage, and if his numbers hold up, he might become the first third-party candidate to do so since Ross Perot in 1992.

Conclusion

In conclusion, the outcome of the 2024 Presidential election will undoubtedly shape the trajectory of the United States in the coming years. The chosen POTUS will face a myriad of challenges and opportunities, and the decisions made during their tenure will significantly impact the nation's future. As citizens engage in the democratic process, it remains essential to prioritize informed decision-making and civic participation to ensure a resilient and prosperous future for the country.